INTERDIMENSIONAL

A PHOTOGRAPHIC TRAVEL LOG

TREVOR RAAB

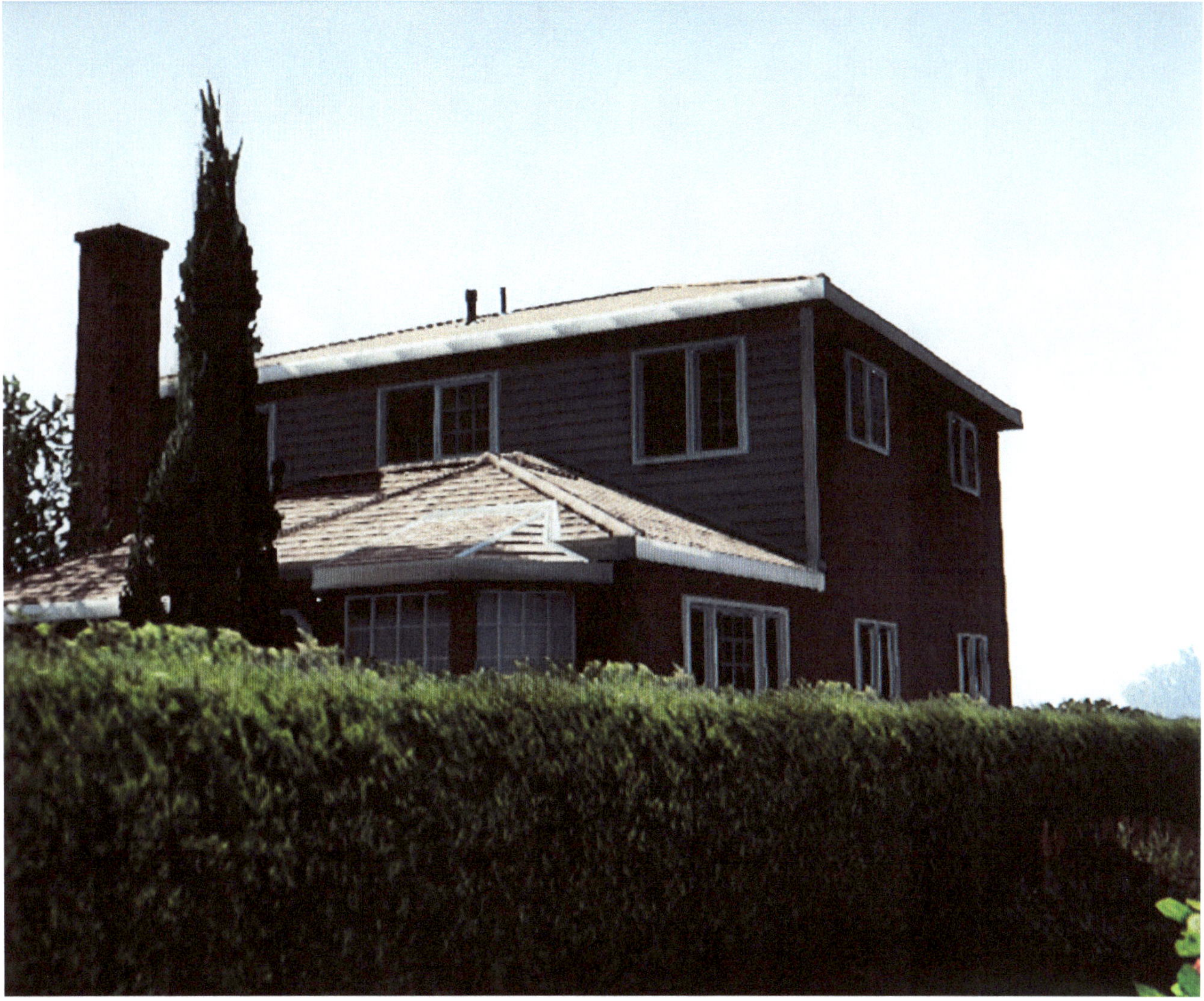

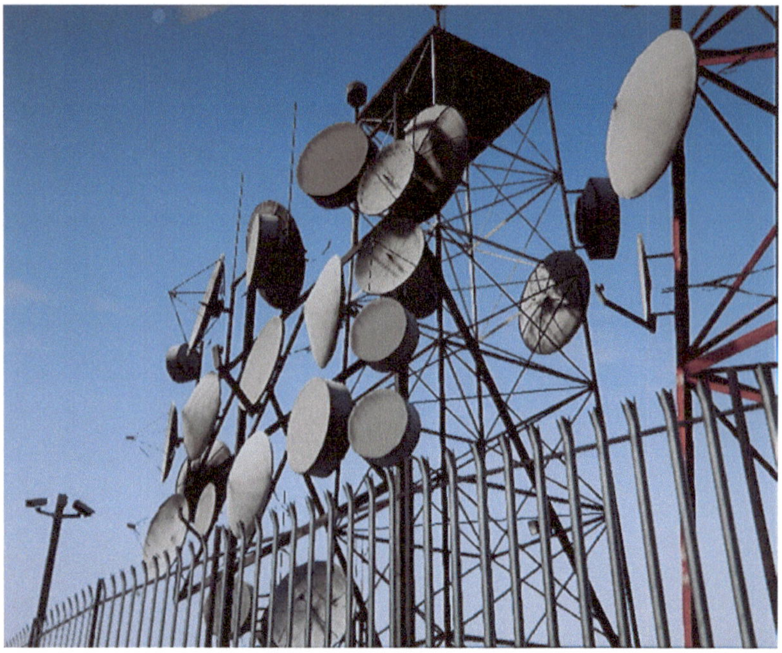

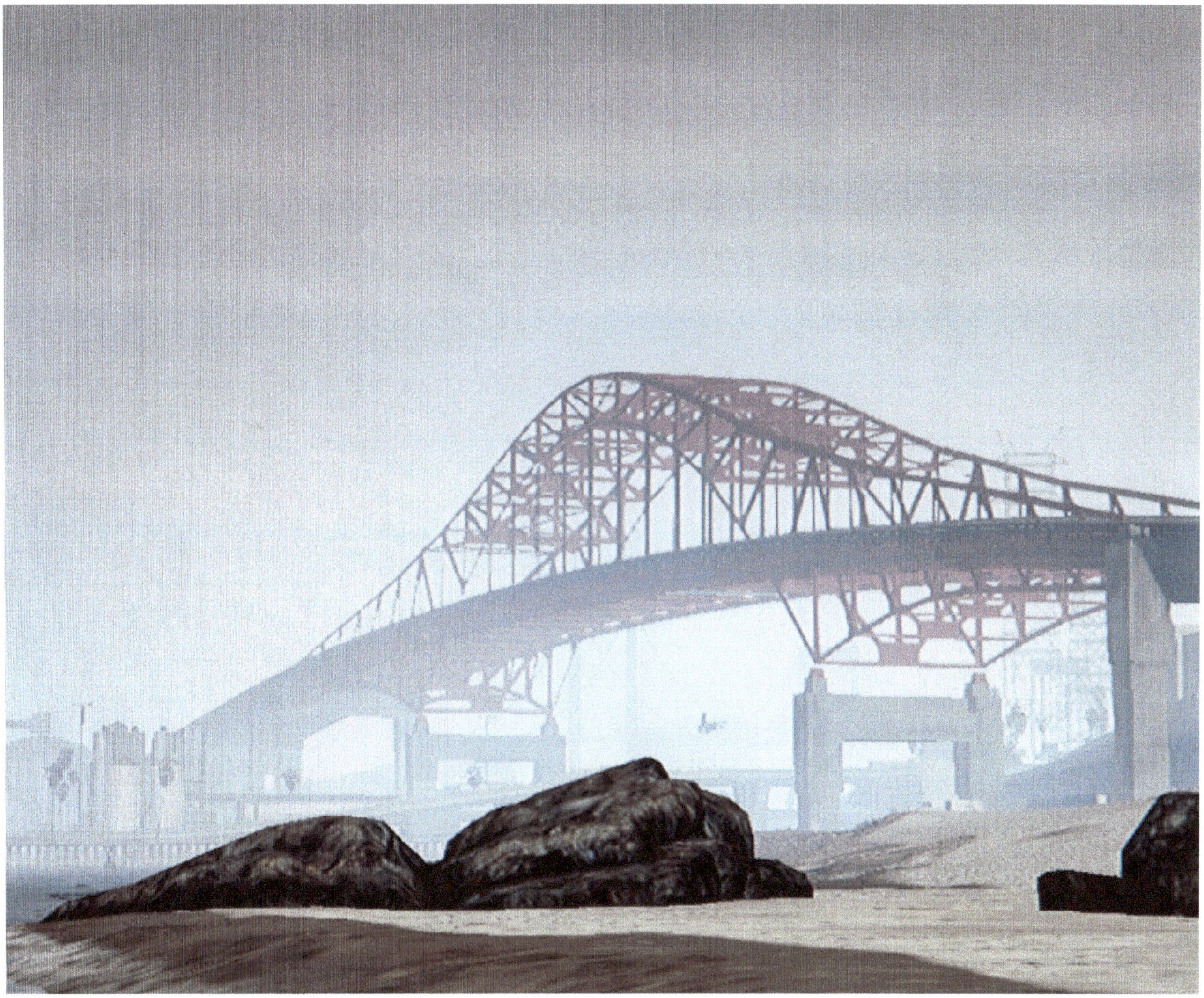

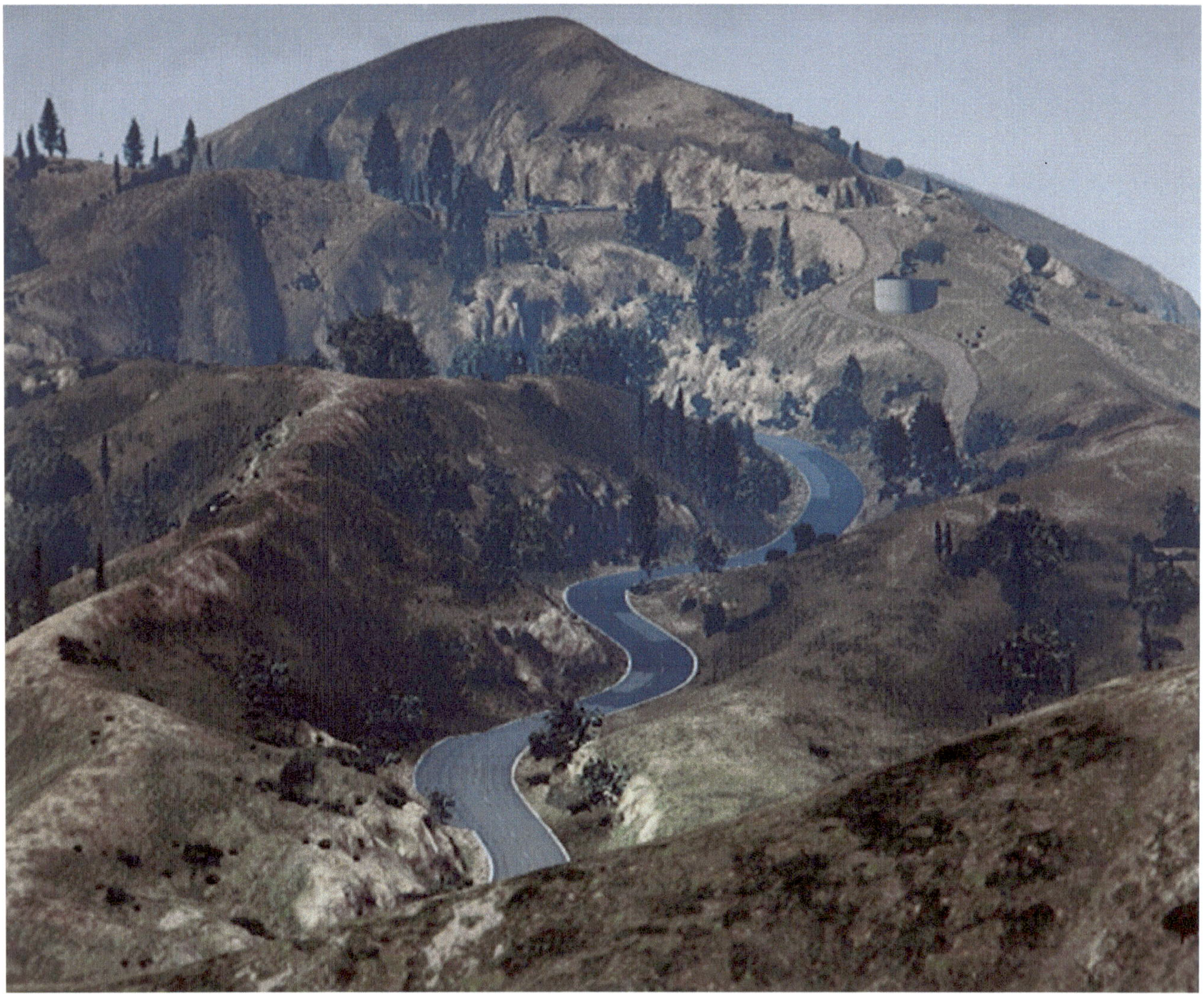

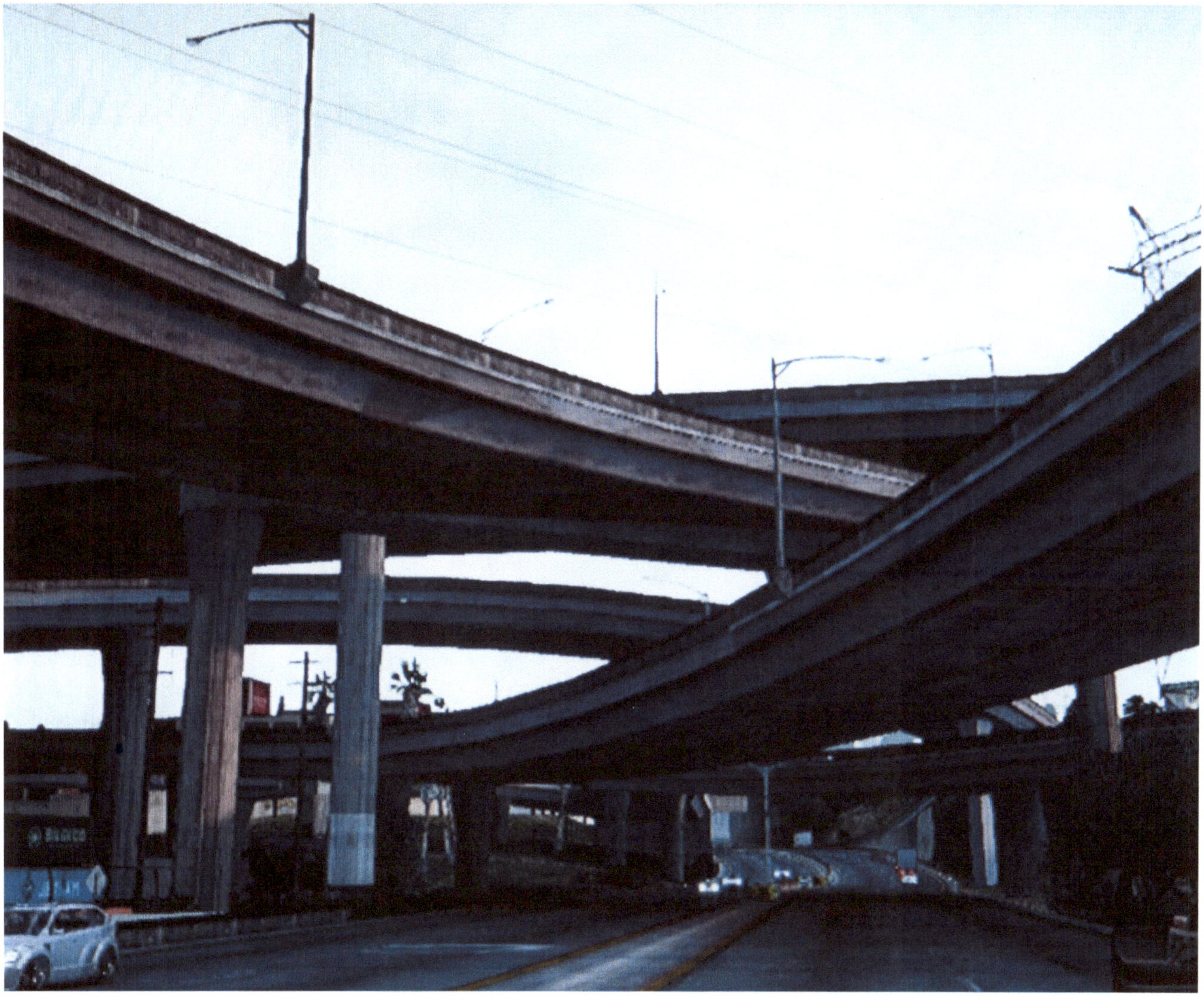

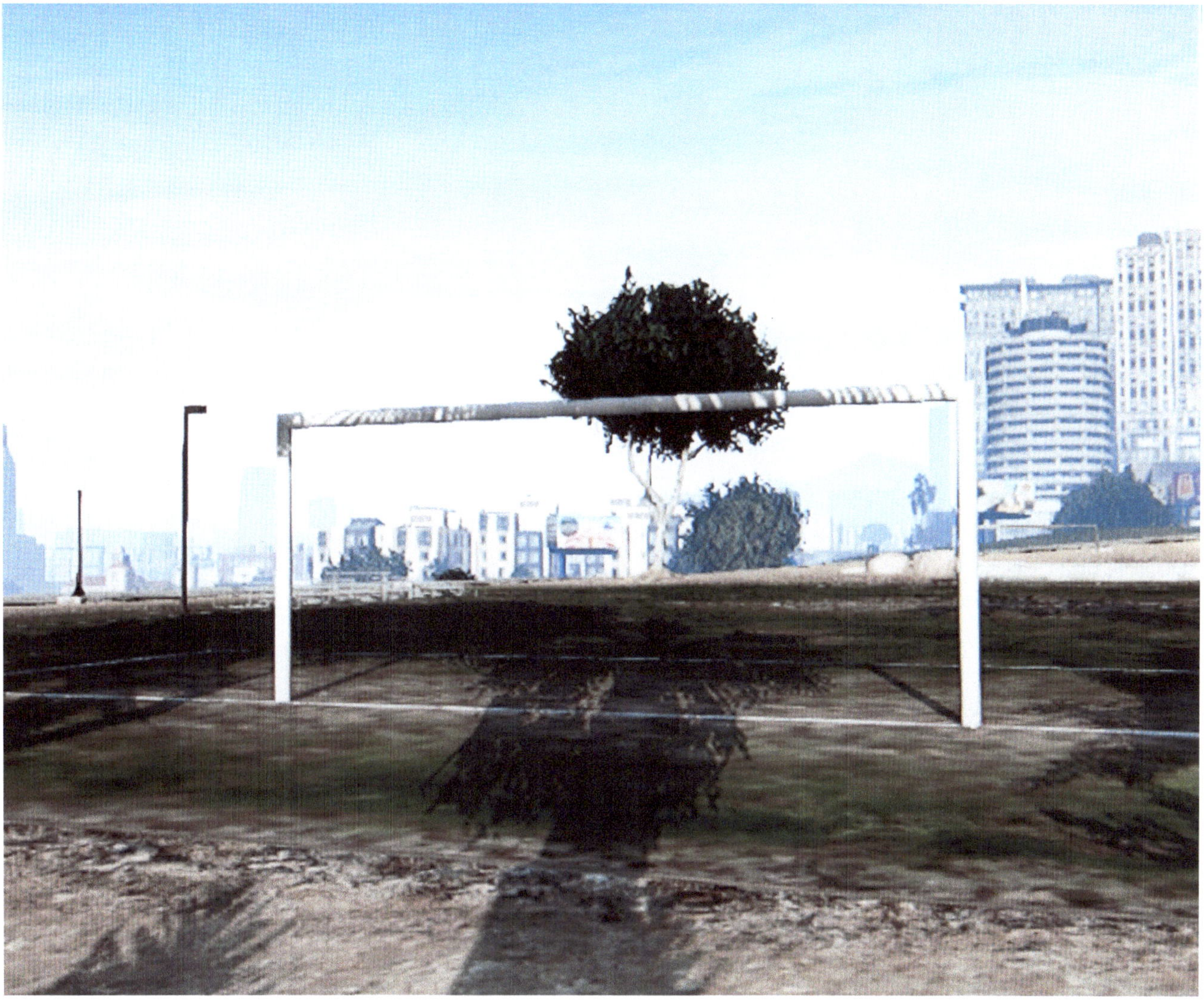

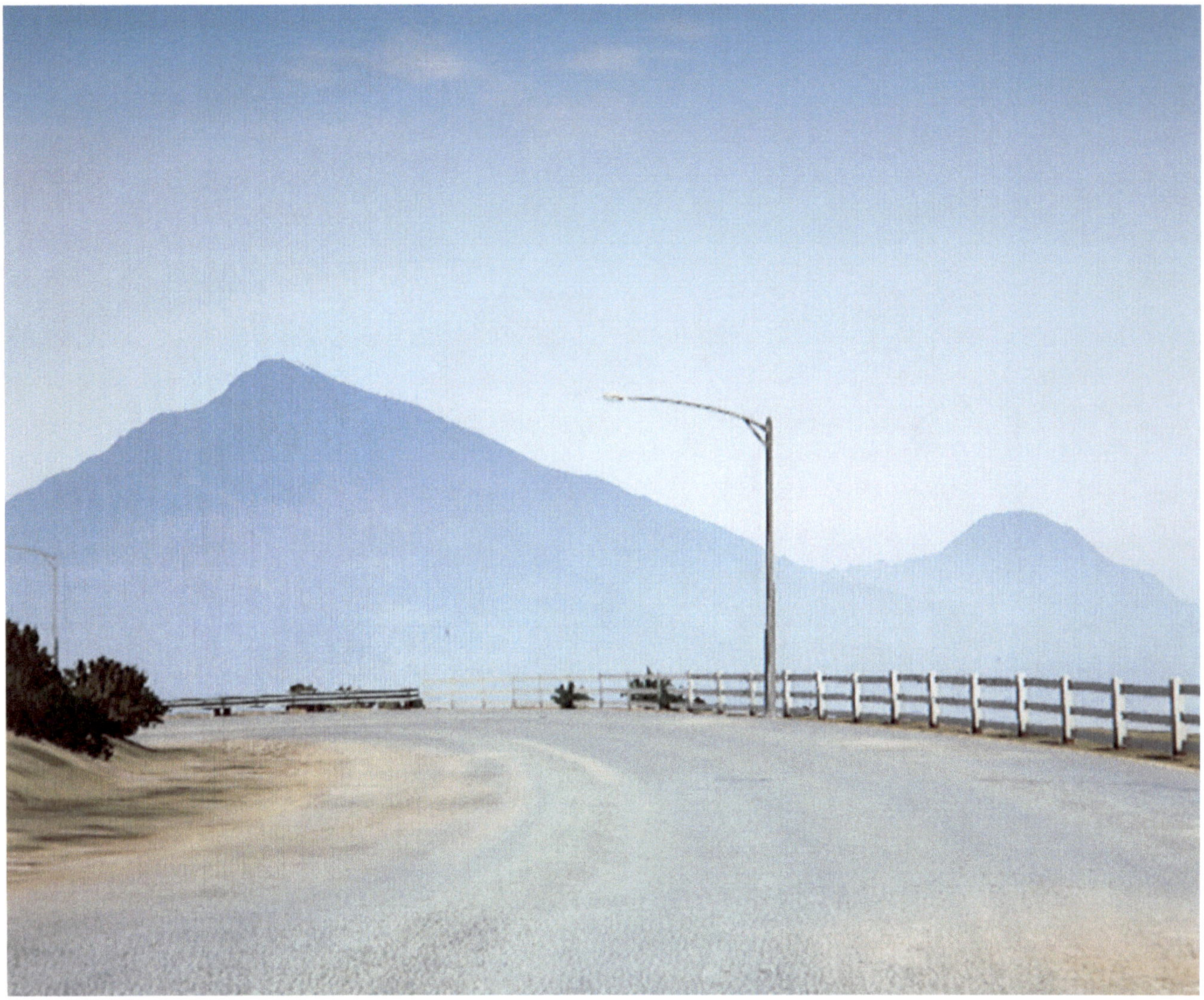

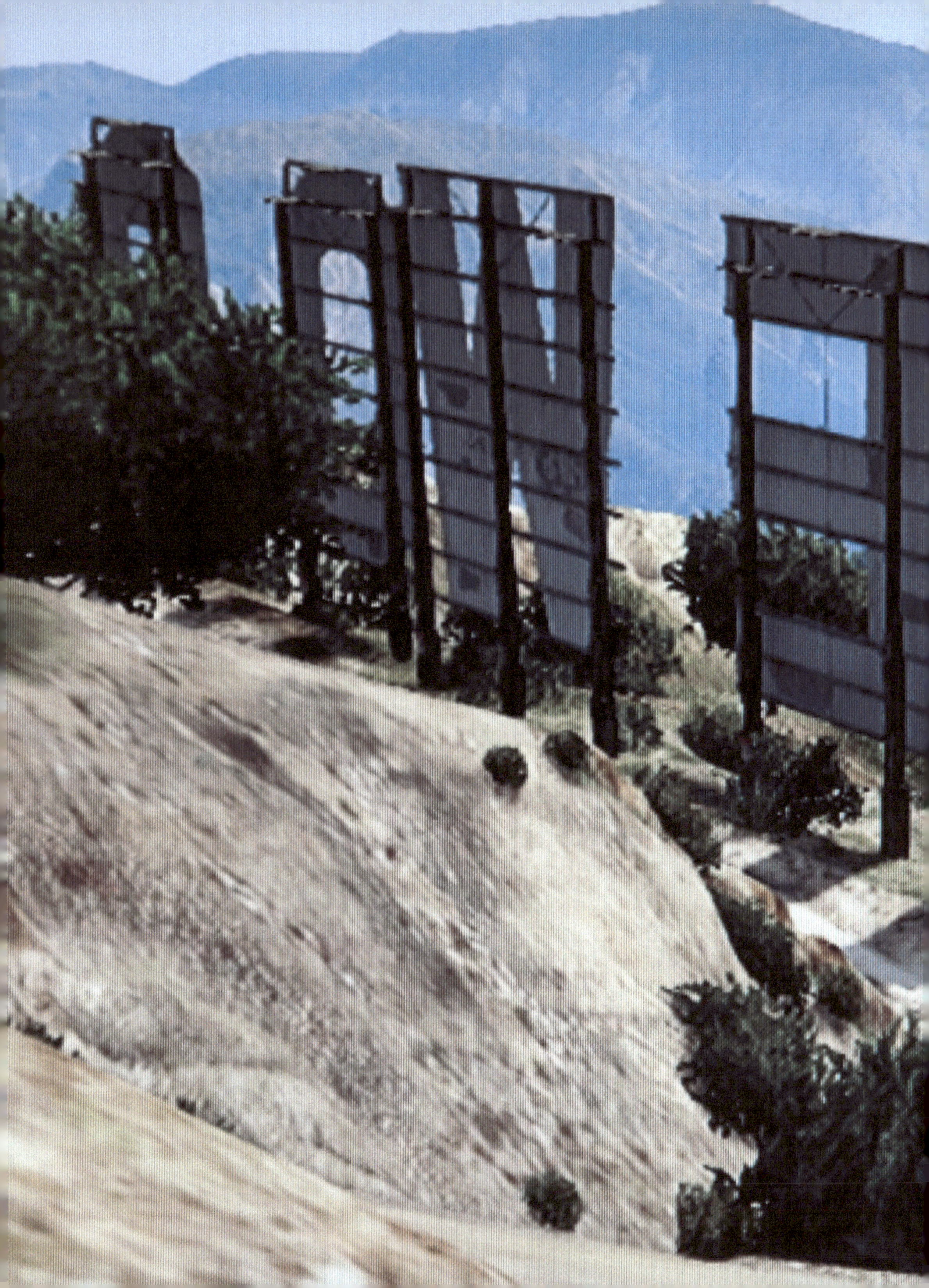

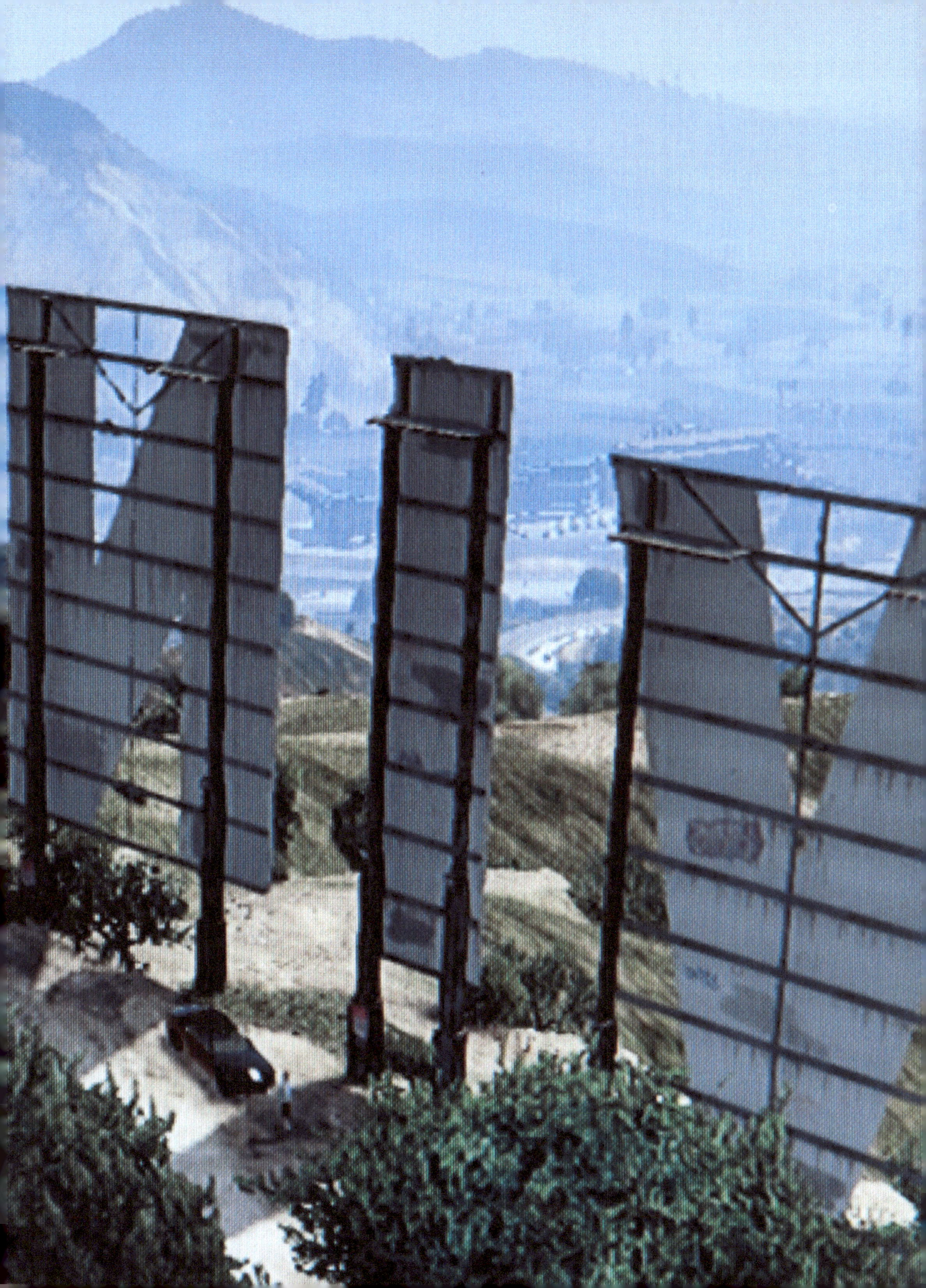

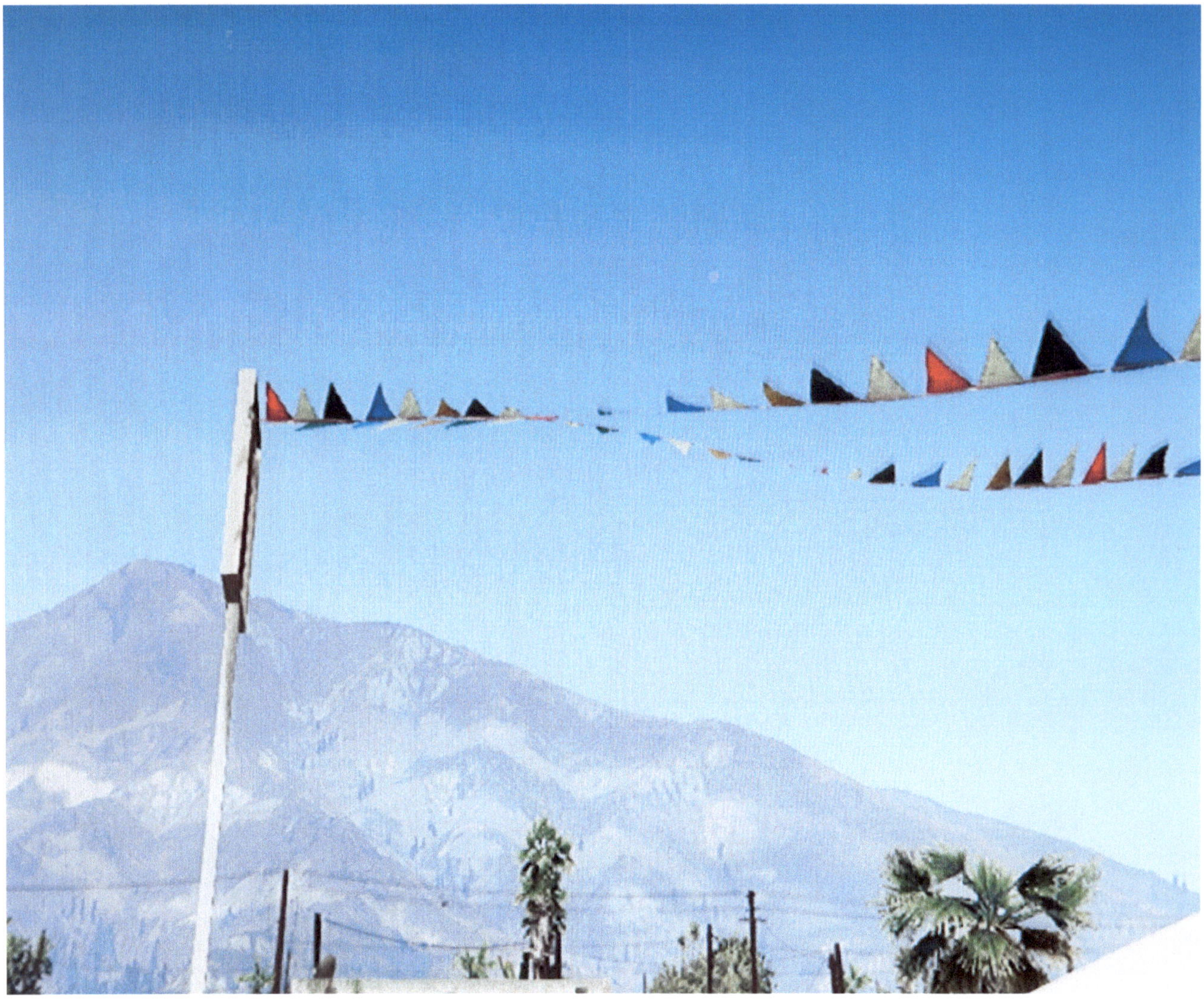

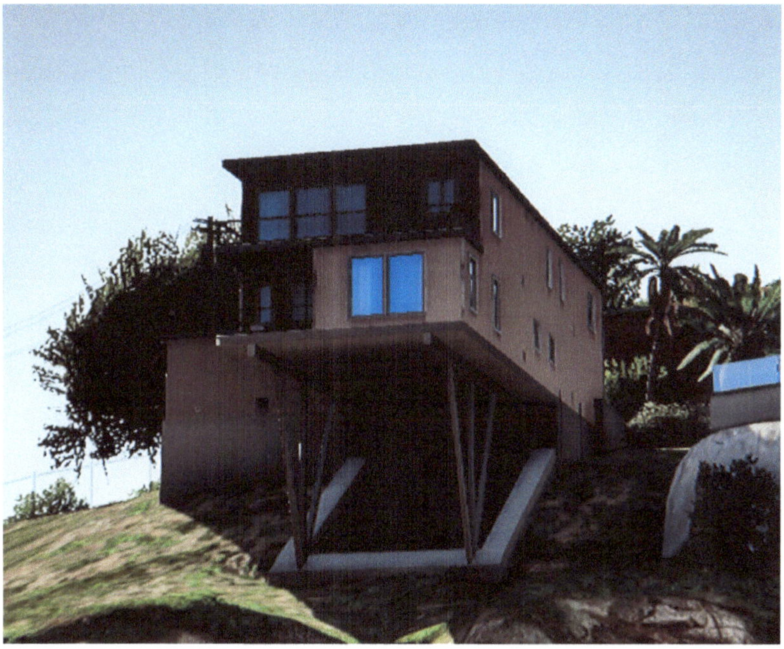

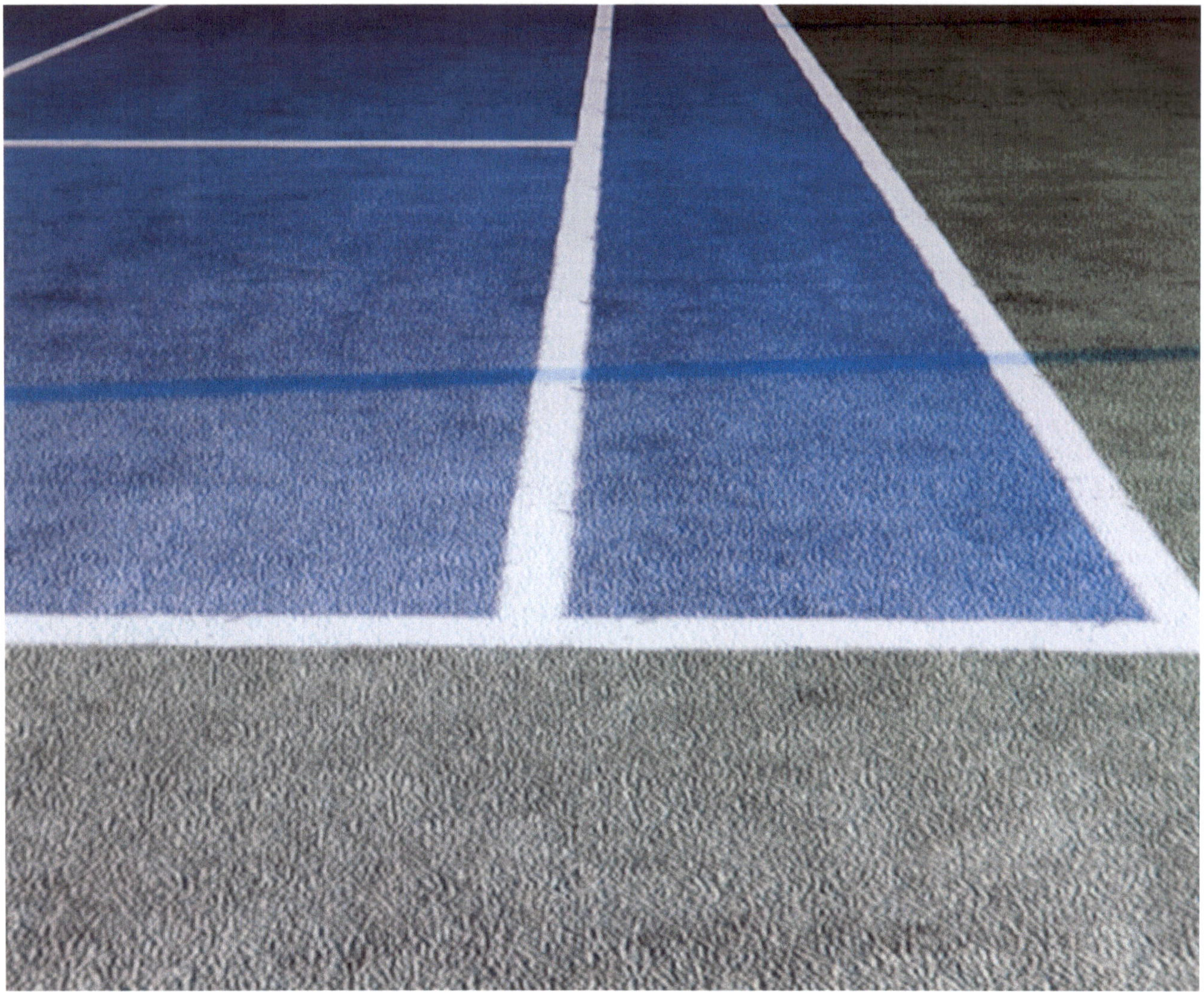

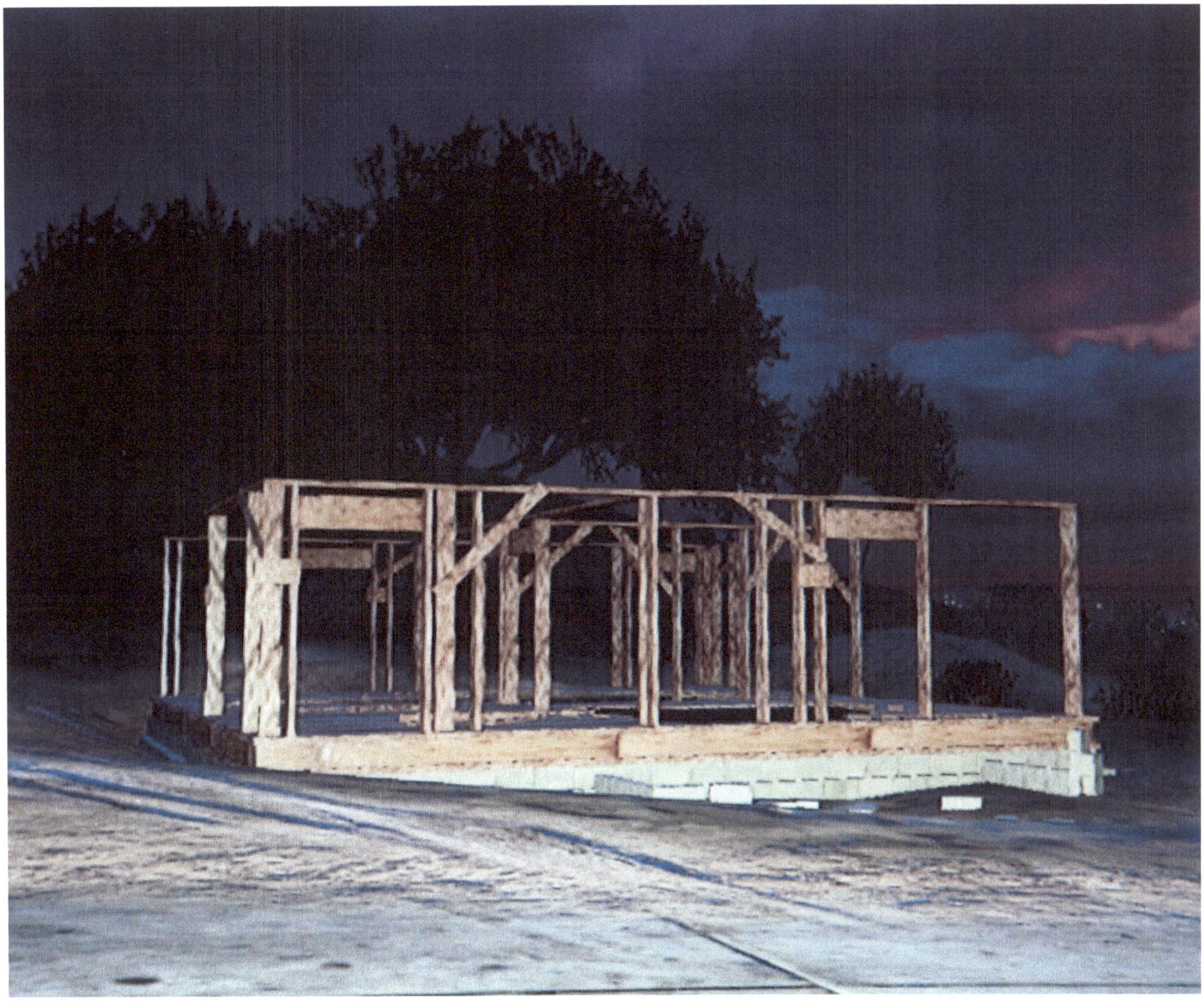

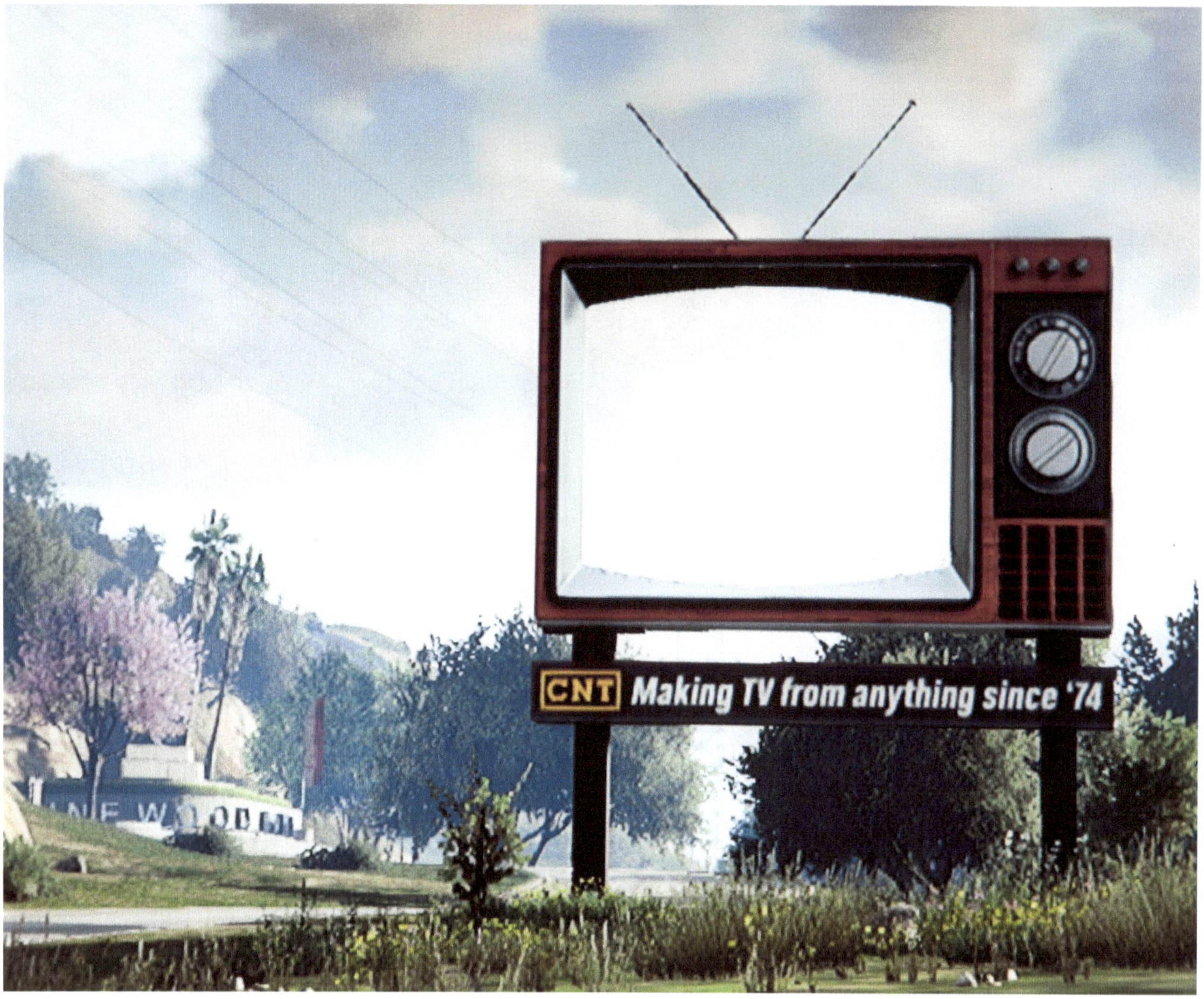
CNT
Making TV from anything since '74

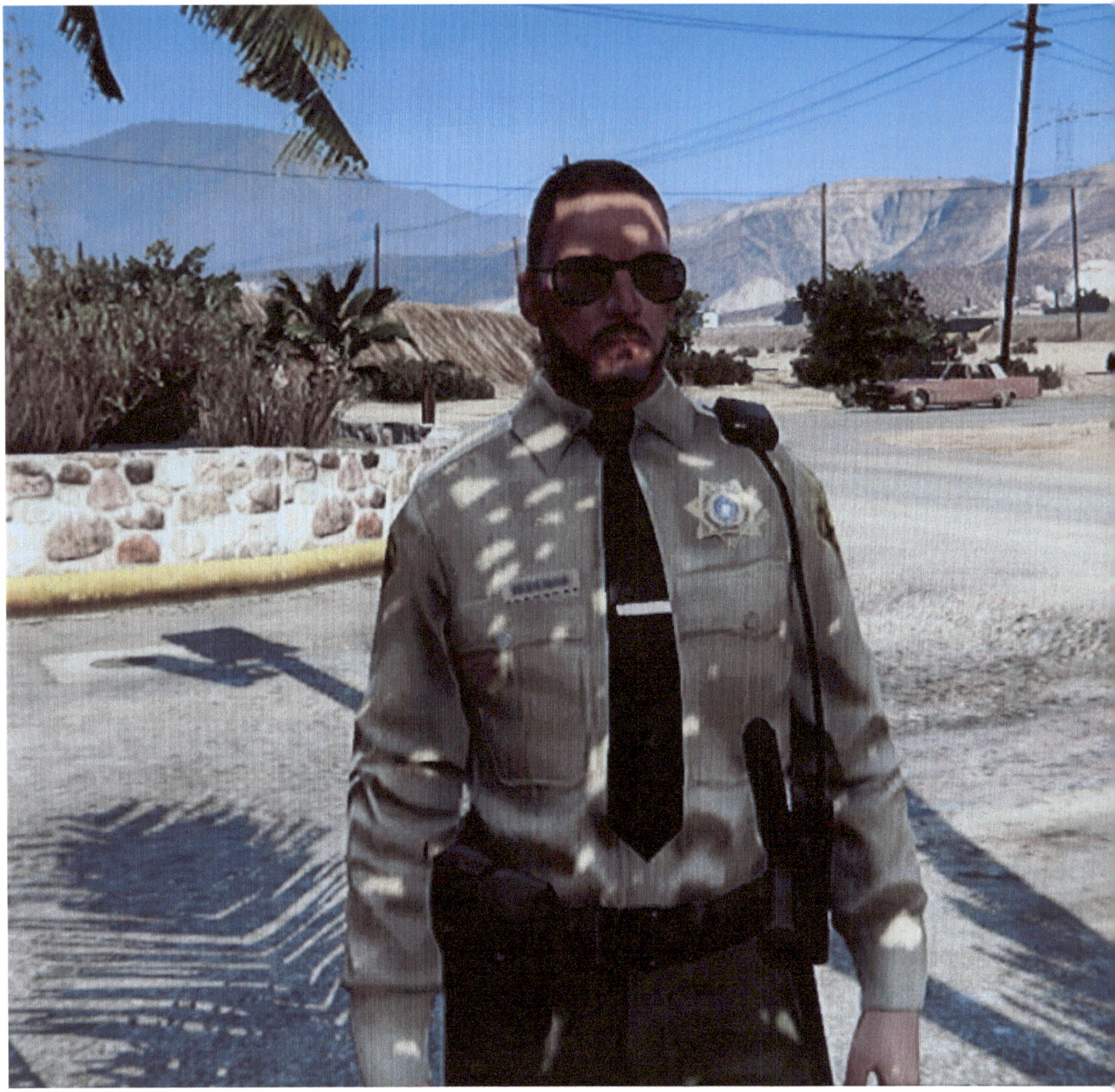

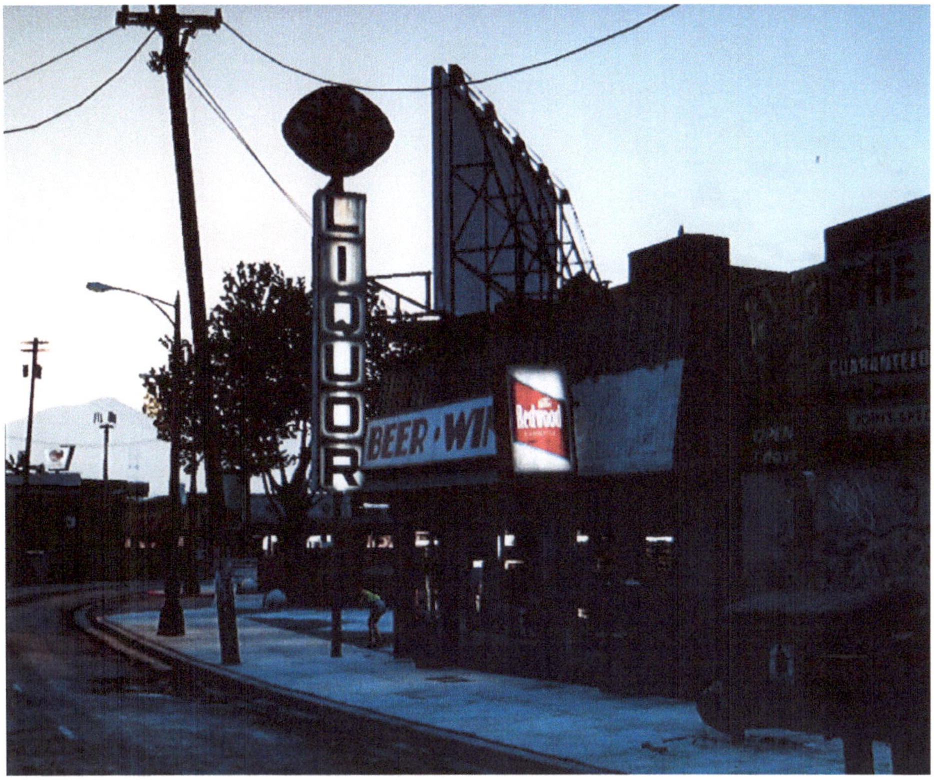
LIQUOR
BEER · WI
Redwood

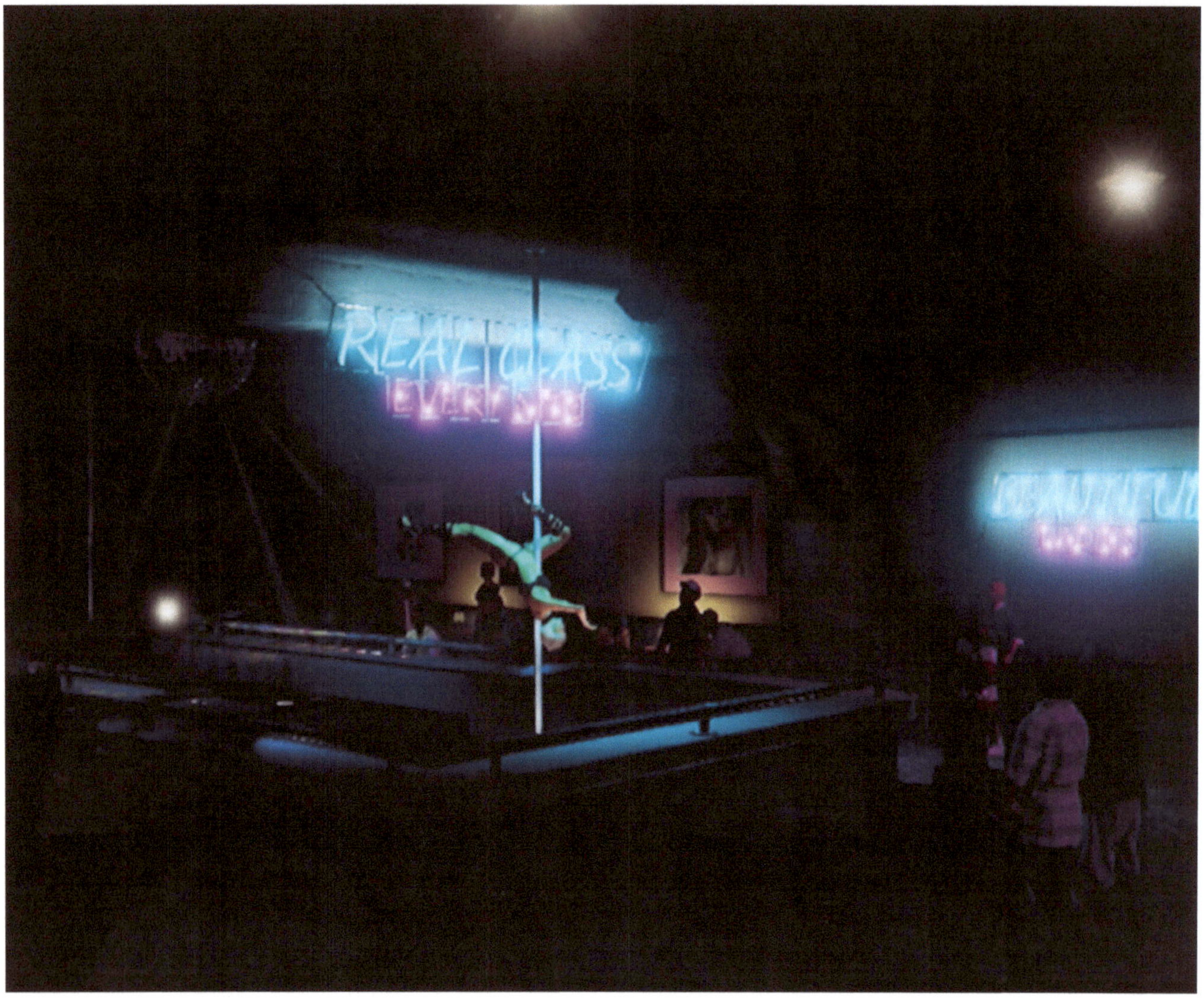
REAL CLASS

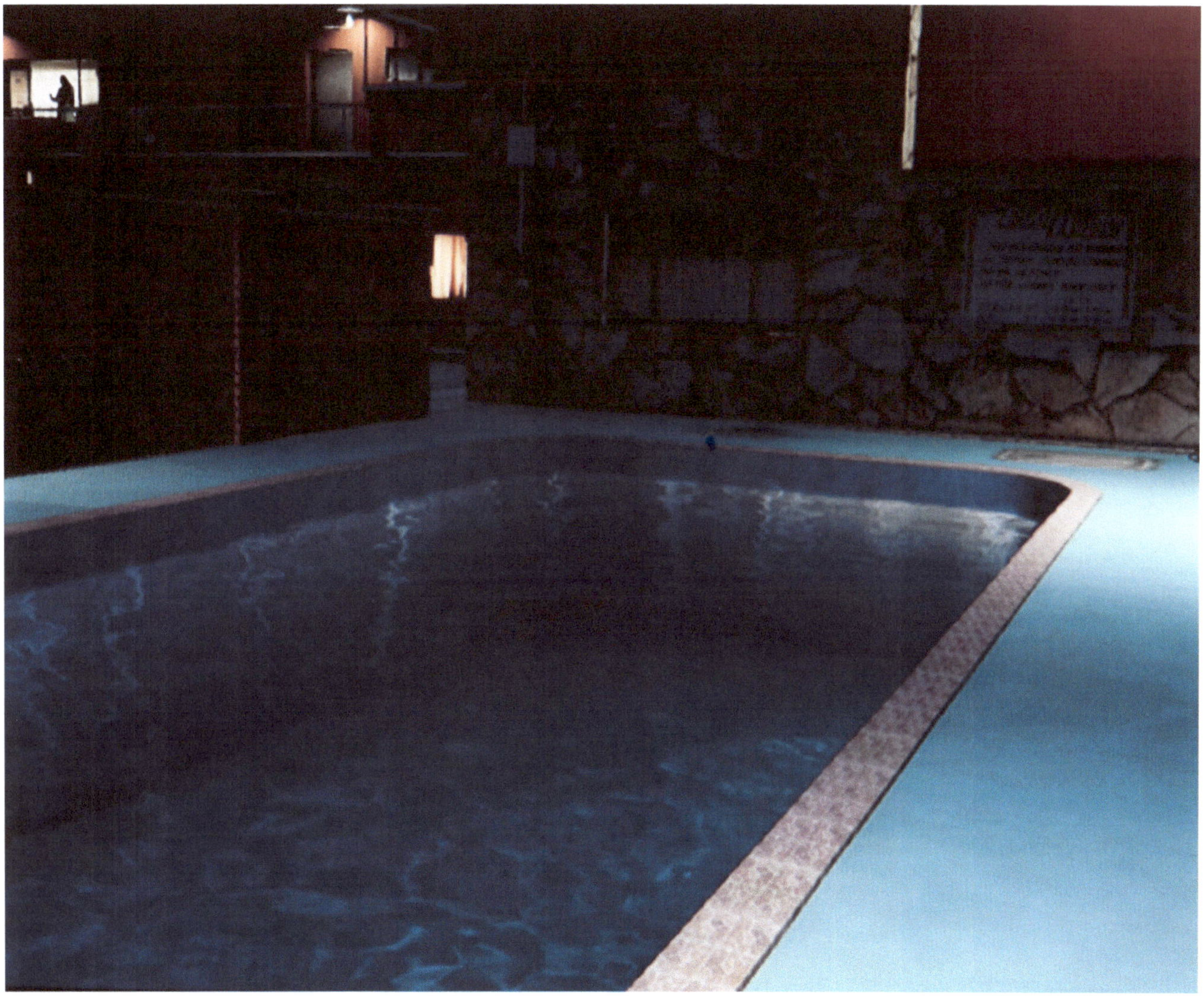

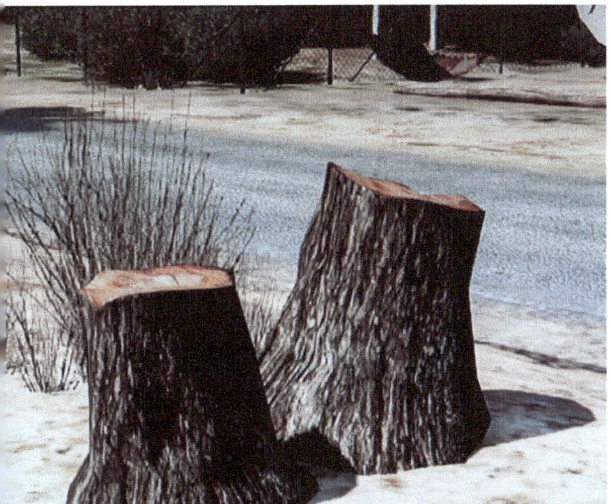

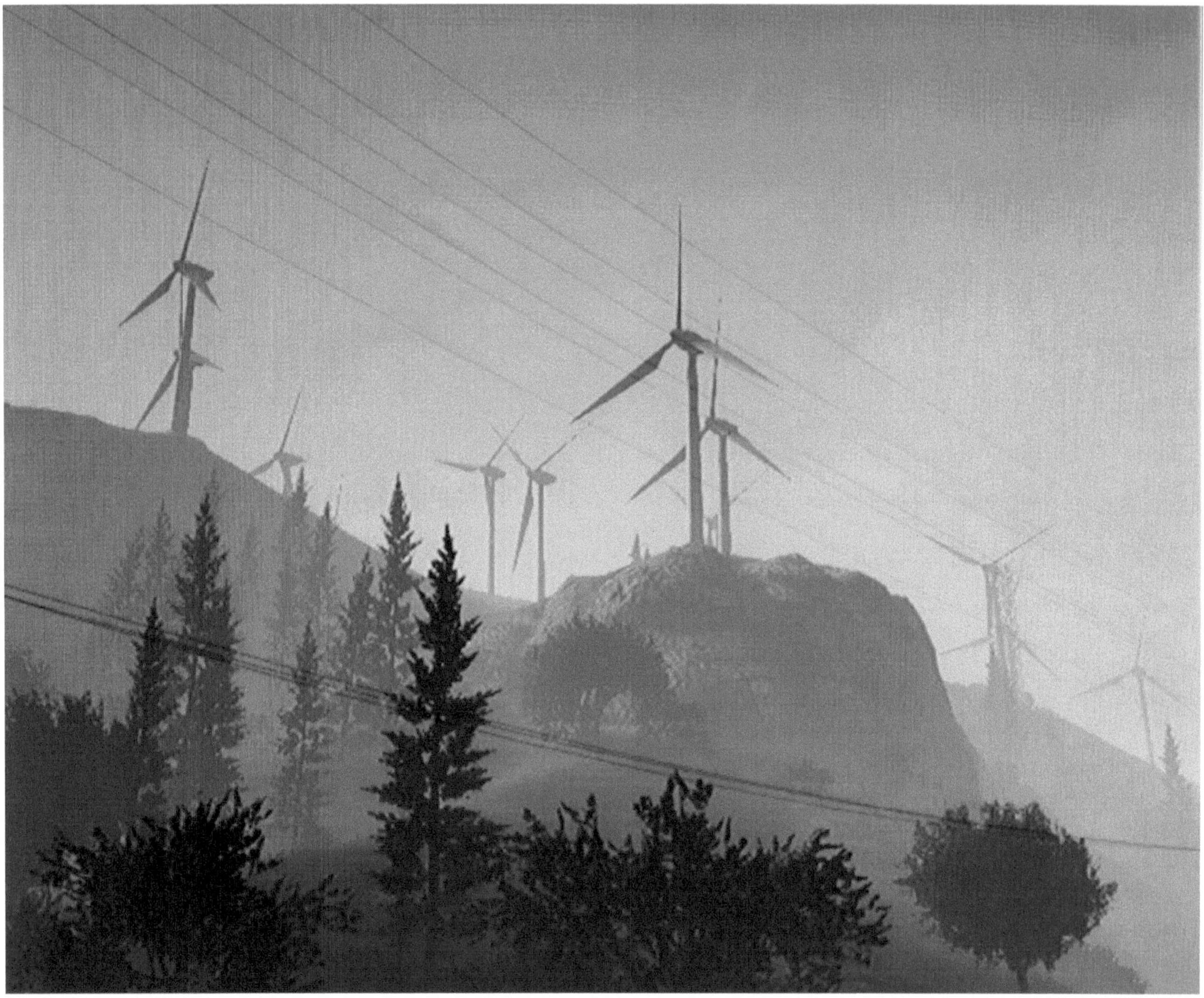

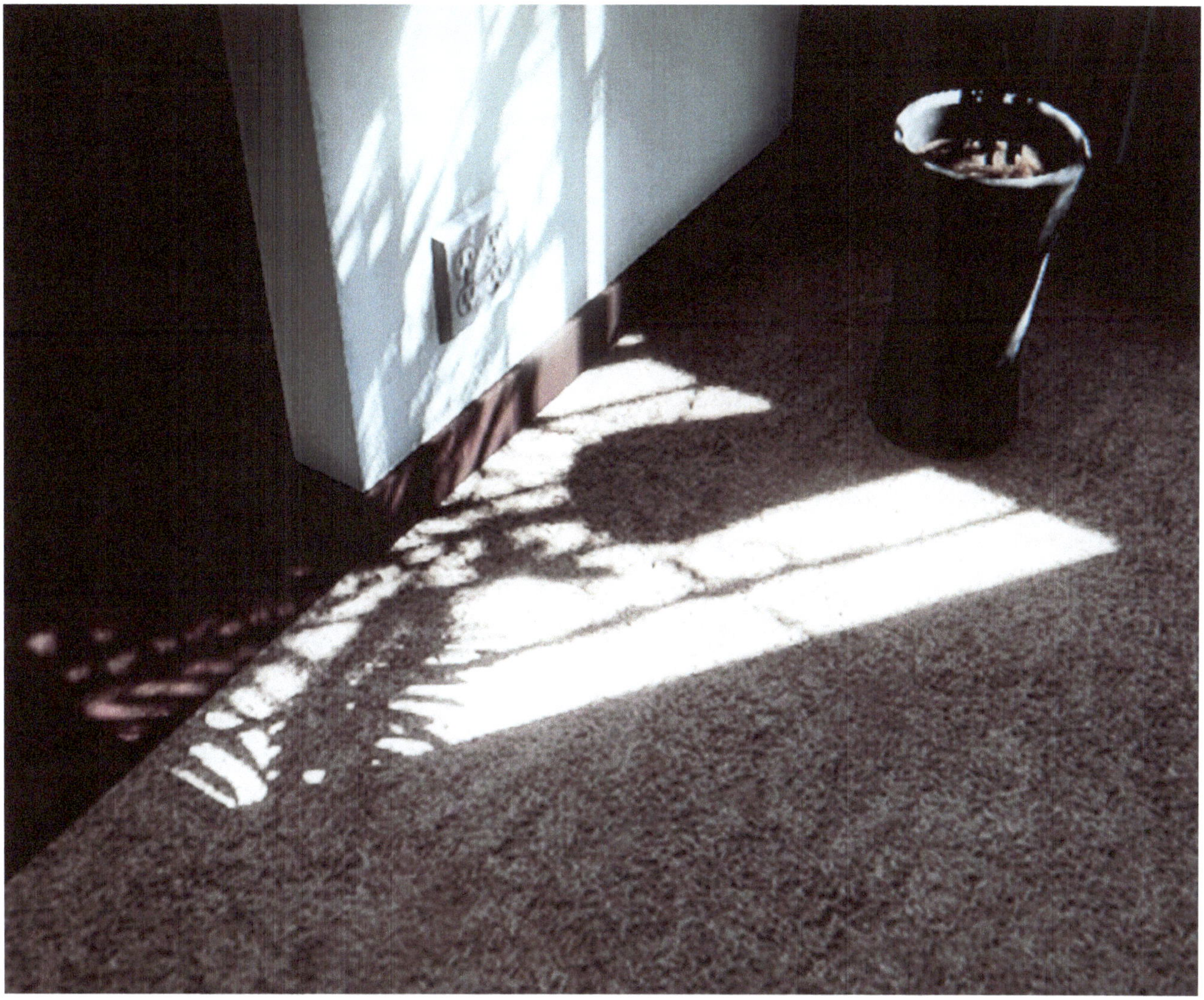

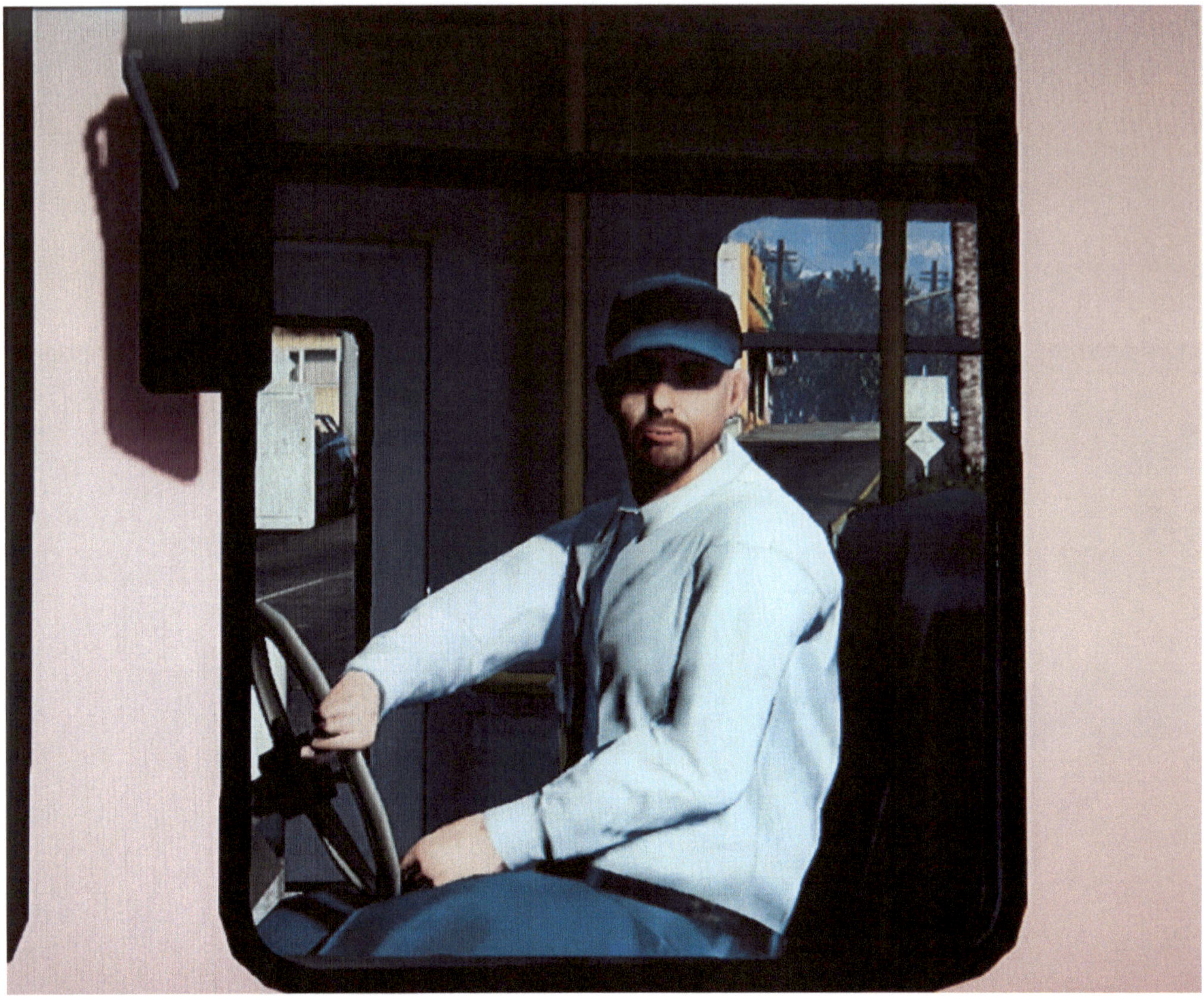

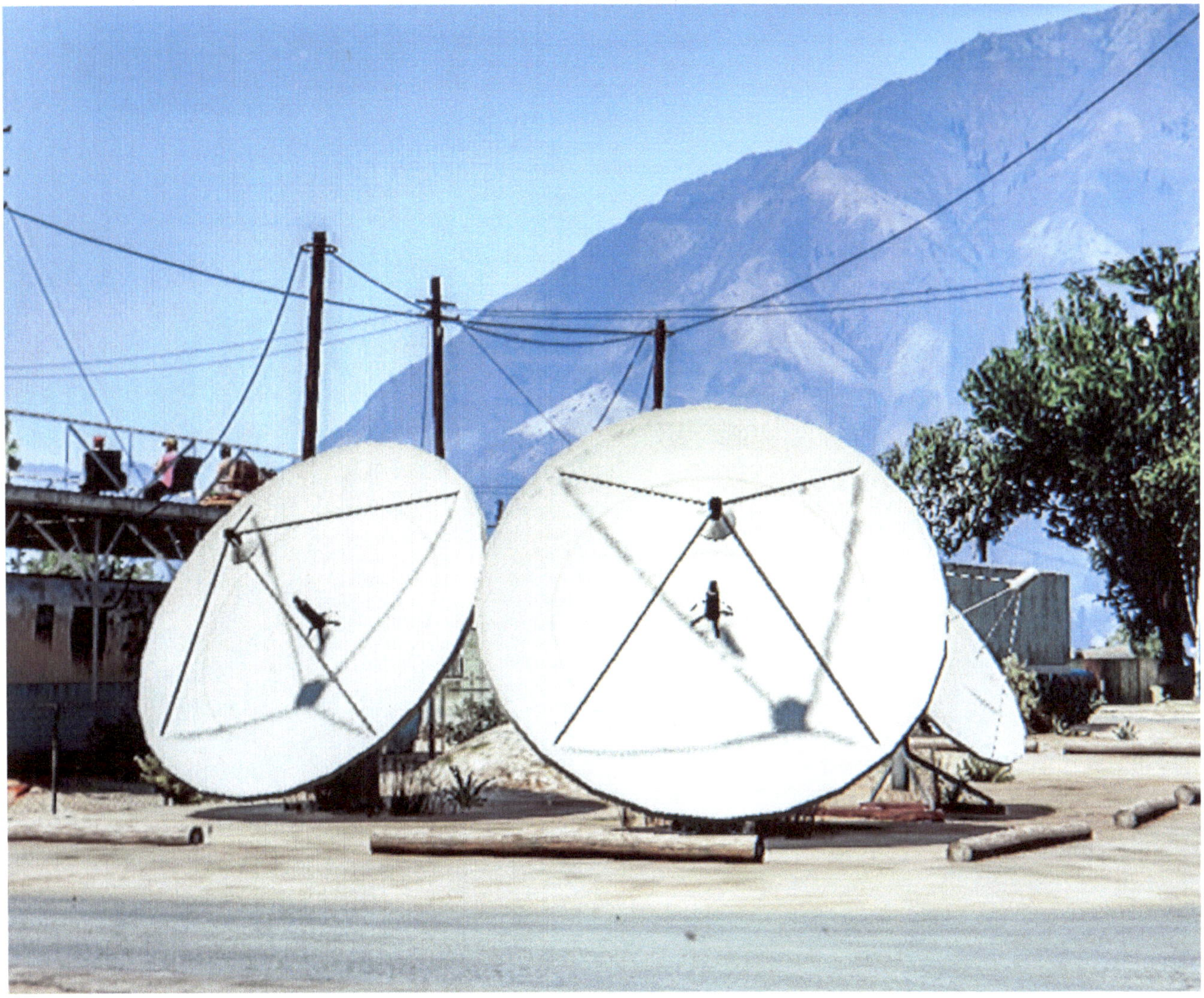

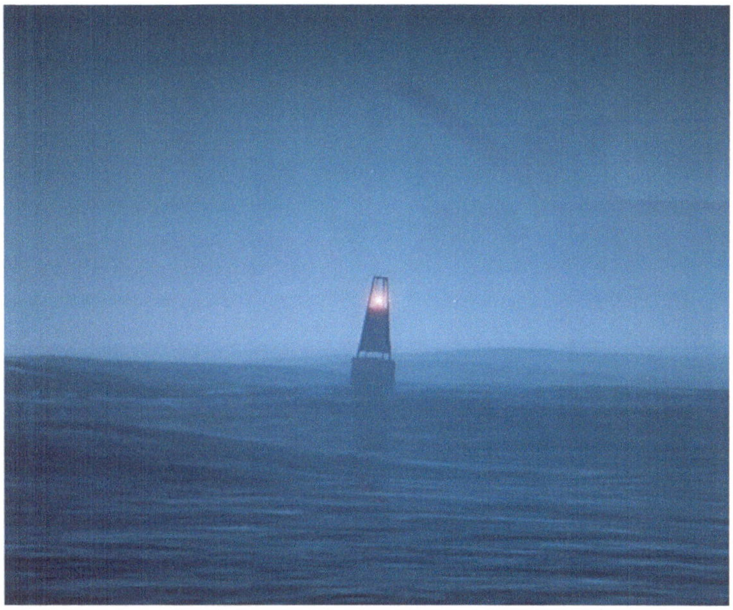

www.ingramcontent.com/pod-product-compliance
Lightning Source LLC
Chambersburg PA
CBHW050904180526
45159CB00007B/2786